LET'S GET SILLY!

Terrific Tongue Twisters

over 30 tongue twisters!

SHE SEES CHEESE

BY CAITIE MCANENEY

WOW!

NEAR AN EAR,
A NEARER EAR,
A NEARLY EERIE EAR

OH MY!

WINDMILL BOOKS

Published in 2025 by Windmill Books, an Imprint of Rosen Publishing
2544 Clinton St., Buffalo, NY 14224

Copyright © 2025 by The Rosen Publishing Group, Inc.

All rights reserved. No part of this book may be reproduced in any form without permission in writing from the publisher, except by a reviewer.

First Edition

Editor: Caitie McAneney
Book Design: Claire Zimmermann

Photo Credits: Series art (cover and interior illustrations) Huza Studio/Shutterstock.com; cover and interior (orange background) elena_l/Shutterstock.com; cover, p. 1 (girl at top) jesadaphorn/Shutterstock.com; cover, p. 1 (ear) Alexander_P/Shutterstock.com; series art (biege background) Q3kiaPictures/Shutterstock.com; p. 5 AI Generated/Shutterstock.com; p. 6 (jars) Drawlab19/Shutterstock.com; p. 7 KRIACHKO OLEKSII/Shutterstock.com; p. 9 Fran Rodriguez Fotografia/Shutterstock.com; p. 11 RLS Photo/Shutterstock.com; p. 13 wavebreakmedia/Shutterstock.com; p. 15 Maryna_Auramchuk/Shutterstock.com; pp. 16 (sneaker), 20 (basketball) kichikimi/Shutterstock.com; p. 17 Denis Moskvinov/Shutterstock.com; p. 19 Jay Ondreicka/Shutterstock.com; p. 20 (bike) runLenarun/Shutterstock.com; p. 21 Roman Samborskyi/Shutterstock.com.

Some of the images in this book illustrate individuals who are models. The depictions do not imply actual situations or events.

Library of Congress Cataloging-in-Publication Data

Names: McAneney, Caitie, author.
Title: Terrific tongue twisters / Caitie McAneney.
Description: Buffalo, NY : Windmill Books, 2025. | Series: Let's get silly! | Includes index.
Identifiers: LCCN 2024025352 (print) | LCCN 2024025353 (ebook) | ISBN 9781538397909 (library binding) | ISBN 9781538397893 (paperback) | ISBN 9781538397916 (ebook)
Subjects: LCSH: Tongue twisters–Juvenile literature. | Plays on words–Juvenile literature. | Wit and humor, Juvenile. | LCGFT: Tongue twisters. | Humor.
Classification: LCC PN6371.5 .M388 2025 (print) | LCC PN6371.5 (ebook) | DDC 818/.602–dc23/eng/20240611
LC record available at https://lccn.loc.gov/2024025352
LC ebook record available at https://lccn.loc.gov/2024025353

Manufactured in the United States of America

CPSIA Compliance Information: Batch #CWWM25. For further information, contact Rosen Publishing at 1-800-237-9932

Contents

What's a Tongue Twister? 4

That's a Mouthful! 6

Water World 8

Silly Sounds 10

School Sketches 12

Short and Silly 14

Longer Twisters 16

Twisted Animals 18

On the Move 20

Glossary 22

For More Information 23

Index 24

Words in the glossary appear in bold
the first time they are used in the text.

What's a Tongue Twister?

Peter Piper picked a peck of pickled peppers.

WOW!

This is an example of a tongue twister. Tongue twisters are word pairs, phrases, or sentences that are hard to say. They often use rhymes and **alliteration**. Some challenge your brain. Some challenge the way your tongue moves. They can help people with speech. Try to say them five times fast!

That's a Mouthful!

Greg grabs green grapes.

Etta ate ample apples.

Jilly juggles jelly jars.

 Peter packs a peanut butter ball.

Fun Fact
Green grapes can taste sour, while purple grapes taste sweet.

Water World

Shelly is a selfish shellfish.

Whales swim, sail's whim

Sadie sells seashells by the seashore.

Swim, swans, swim!
Seven swans swam.
Well swum, swans!

Fun Fact
Shellfish include crustaceans like lobsters and shrimp, as well as clams and octopi.

Silly Sounds

The witch wears a Swiss wristwatch.

The gargoyle wears argyle.

Benny the anemone sees an enemy anemone.

TEEHEE!

Busy Lizzy was in a tizzy. If she weren't in a tizzy, would Lizzy be busy?

Fun Fact
Anemones may look like underwater plants, but they're actually meat-eating sea creatures!

School Sketches

A flute tutor tooted her flute to teach two tired tooters to toot. ♪

Miss Sissy's socks show shocking spots.

Mister Marks makes math matter.

Sheena shares her science sheet.

12

Fun Fact 🎵
People who play the flute are called flutists or flautists.

Short and Silly

Winnie's really weary.

WHOA! Specific Pacific

red lorry, yellow lorry

Fun Fact
"Lorry" is a British word for a truck, or a vehicle made to carry loads.

bad money, mad bunny

15

Longer Twisters

A bug bit a big bat, but the big bat bit the bug back.

If your dog chews shoes, which shoes would she choose?

Fun Fact
The biggest bat on Earth is the giant flying fox. Its wingspan can be up to 5 feet (1.5 m).

CeCe went to sea,
to see the sea that she could see.
The sea she saw was a shiny sea,
a sort of shiny sea saw she.

Twisted Animals

Red fox fed rocks.

Sheep should sleep on sheets.

The snake snuck some seltzer for his snack.

A skunk sat on a step and thunk the step stunk, but the step thunk the skunk stunk.

Fun Fact
The sharp smell from a skunk's oily spray can last for days.

19

On the Move

Winn ran in warm rain.

She threw three free throws.

bad Mike
mad bike

🏀 Fun Fact

In basketball, a free throw is a basket made from behind a certain line. It can earn a player one point.

Greg moves, Meg grooves.

Glossary

alliteration: The repetition of the same sound at the beginning of words in a phrase or sentence.

anemone: A sea creature called a polyp whose shape and bright colors resemble a flower.

argyle: A diamond-shaped pattern of two or more colors, most often seen on knit pieces of clothing.

gargoyle: A sculpture of an odd or ugly animal or person carved as a decoration on a building.

specific: Certain.

weary: Tired in body and mind.

whim: A sudden desire or change in mind.

For More Information

BOOKS

Panz, S. Marty. *The Giant Joke Book for Kids.* Chicago, IL: Sequoia Children's Publishing, 2024.

Pattison, Rosie Gowsell. *Just Joking 7.* Washington, D.C.: National Geographic, 2022.

Tongue Twisters! Honesdale, PA: Highlights Press, 2022.

WEBSITES

Kids Tongue Twisters
www.ducksters.com/tonguetwisters.php
Explore more fun tongue twisters with Ducksters!

Tongue Twisters for Kids
www.playosmo.com/kids-learning/tongue-twisters-for-kids/
Discover new tongue twisters, and learn why they're so important for speech.

Publisher's note to educators and parents: Our editors have carefully reviewed these websites to ensure that they are suitable for students. Many websites change frequently, however, and we cannot guarantee that a site's future contents will continue to meet our high standards of quality and educational value. Be advised that students should be closely supervised whenever they access the internet.

Index

alliteration, 4

anemones, 10, 11

basketball, 20

bats, 16

brain, 4

Earth, 16

flute, 12, 13

grapes, 7

math, 12

phrases, 4

rhymes, 4

science, 12

sea, 8, 11, 17

shellfish, 8, 9

skunks, 18, 19

speech, 4

tongue, 4